A Special Gift

PRESENTED TO

FROM

DATE

CELEBRATING THE INNER BEAUTY OF WOMAN

Copyright © 1998
Janette Oke

Published by Bethany House Publishers
A Ministry of Bethany Fellowship, Inc.
11300 Hampshire Avenue South
Minneapolis, Minnesota 55438

Art Direction & Design: Lookout Design Group, Minneapolis, MN   (www.lookoutdesign.com)

Photography (jacket & interior except where noted):
 Studio: Dietrich Gesk, Minneapolis, MN
 Makeup & Hair: Randee Paster
 Wardrobe & Prop Stylist: Janna Noel

 6, 20, 34, 46, 48, 62, 80, 85: Lookout Design Group
 35, 63, 69, 81: Kim & Peggy Warmoltz, Tarpon Springs, Florida
 12, 13: Photodisc, Inc.
 7: Romilly Lockyer
 21: Elyse Lewin
 29: David De Lossy
 49: Maria Taglienti
 61: Sonja/An Bullaty/Lomeo

Special Thanks:
 James A. Mulvey House, Stillwater, MN
 James H. Clark House, Excelsior, MN

Printed in China

Library of Congress Cataloging-in-Publication Data

Oke, Janette, 1935-
 Celebrating the inner beauty of woman / by Janette Oke.
 p. cm.
 ISBN 0-7642-2041-1 (pbk.)
 1. Women—Religious life. 2. Christian life. I. Title.
BV4527.O34   1998
242'.643—dc21
                                            97-45437
                                            CIP

JANETTE OKE

Celebrating
THE INNER BEAUTY
OF Woman

BETHANY HOUSE PUBLISHERS
MINNEAPOLIS, MINNESOTA 55438

Beauty

is not only in the
creamy cheek,
the well-formed brow,
the freshness of
the face of youth.

Beauty

is of the heart,
the soul,
that reaches out
to grace
the world with...

STRENGTH, LOVE, KINDNESS,
COMPASSION, DEVOTION, & TENDERNESS

The Beauty
OF STRENGTH

STRENGTH

What does it take to be strong?
Most of all a sharing of strength with strength
knowing that real strength
comes from the joining of hearts and hands.

Let us *Laugh* together

Listen to one another's words

Lean on one another's strength

Love one another from an honest heart.

Then nothing we face will seem

TOO BIG for us to overcome.

The future can be

as bright as the

Colors

we choose to hold

in our hands.

Your *Smile*

is the light that illumines my day

Your *Gurgle*

the song that gladdens my heart

and the

Clasp of your tiny finger

the bond that holds my world together.

You are

OLDER & WISER

have seen more of life

felt the jolts and jars

that make us weak or strong.

That is why I value

so highly our friendship.

Alone

I do not have

the courage

the strength

the tenacity

to complete the dream.

Together

Each one

reaches

to support

the other.

SON

What is a son?

So much a part of me

and yet so much

the seedling of a man.

❧ ❧ ❧

May I live carefully

so as to impart not so much me

But more of

FATHER GOD.

The Beauty

OF LOVE

If there really were magic it would surely come from

L O V E

For it is love that prompts all good, all noble, all enduring

acts and deeds and thoughts.

Even as you press my hand
then pass it to another

I see the LOVE
shine in your eyes

and I know that though I am
this new man's WIFE

and SOUL MATE
I will always be to you your

Little Girl

She lights a

CANDLE

puts it on the table's snowy lace

it makes the crystal sparkle

shadows dance

She dims the lights

and checks the roast

straightens her hair

Her new groom's coming home.

You were always there
whenever I needed a listening ear
or just a good giggle

when I felt
Down or Up

when I wanted to bare my soul
or hang on to my silence.

I guess that's what sisters are for.

❧ ❧ ❧

Tomorrow

seems a

SAFER PLACE

when I walk

toward it

with

YOU

at my side.

Even when

we walk in

S H A D O W S

I feel

much safer

with my hand

in yours.

FRAGILE? Yes.

But strong enough to hold

my world in baby hands.

Bone of my bone

Flesh of my flesh

But even more…

Heartbeat of My Heart.

The Beauty

OF KINDNESS

KINDNESS
is a special language of love spoken in simple acts and deeds,
rich in fluency, and alive with undertones of mystical,
musical good will.

KNOWLEDGE
BEAUTY
GRACE

Thank you

for sharing

so much of yourself

with me.

Sharing

a task

a summer day

a troubled heart.

I have often found

whatever we share

is sweeter when it's shared

with you.

The most

PRECIOUS GIFT

you have given to me

is the knowledge

that I

am not alone.

Woman to Woman

it is nice to sit and chat

to share the day's events

and how we feel

and what makes sense

and how to fix our hair

and if we'll vote the same

again this year.

It's nice to be a woman

and to share

my womanhood with you

My mother-friend.

Little girls

and

Warm Hugs

go so well

together.

Hi, Mom.

Got a minute?

I've got some good news.

And my day is suddenly brighter

for there is no one

I would sooner share good news with

than you.

XOXO

The Beauty
OF COMPASSION

COMPASSION
How can you separate the
word from woman?

Hi, Mom.

Got a minute?

I've got some good news.

And my day is suddenly brighter

for there is no one

I would sooner share good news with

than you.

XOXO

The Beauty

OF COMPASSION

COMPASSION
How can you separate the
word from woman?

❦ ❦ ❦

Walk softly

Mama is sleeping.

She used to caution folks

to hush their noise

while I slept.

Now it is my turn

to think of her.

Shhh....

Does she read my eyes?
Is my smile forced a bit?

Can she see that little ache

within my heart

as I say the proper words

to share her moment of celebration

of new motherhood?

I would not rob her joy or wish her less

than what she holds dear

But my arms ache

to hold a baby of my own.

No one

can understand

the thoughts

and feelings

of a woman

quite like

another woman.

That's why

God gave us...

mothers, sisters, & friends.

I think it was

for this hour,

for this

R E A S O N

that God

sent you into

my life.

A Sister

is a special gift

given by a God

who understands

our need

for someone

who can be even

Closer

than a friend.

THE EMPTY SWING

rocks gently in the breeze

the sandbox only holds
the winter storm

the bike is there
to lose its paint
and gather rust

And as she looks through
eyes with tears

She is reminded with an aching
heart that in some
pain-free yesterday

She was a mother.

The Beauty
OF DEVOTION

DEVOTION
A little part of me,
a little part of him
and oh so much of Heaven

How does a mother express love?

In a million ways.

In tone, in touch, with eyes,

voice, hands, and lips

∓ through DISCIPLINE

∓ and through DEVOTION

∓ by BEING THERE

∓ enfolding close or URGING ON

∓ holding a hand or LETTING GO.

All are a part of the language of LOVE.

HONEYMOON

the whole world is ours

to see and taste

to savor and enjoy

But with a face that bears no blush of shame

I'll tell you this

I can't wait to get home.

OUR HOME.

♥

She laughs

a silvery tinkling bell

She sings

the gladsome heart of the early bluebird

She dances

with the abandonment of innocence

She is mine

and she spontaneously expresses

all the joy I feel inside

each time I look at her.

♥

You were not included in my plan.

But had I missed you

I would have missed so much

for now that you are here

I cannot feel my life

would ever have

been complete…

Without You.

"Guess what?"

It is a favorite game you play

and I am never sure

Just where your fancies might

take us.

But still, I tag along

Knowing I'll discover once again

forgotten wonderment

of things once known.

Tiny

CUPS

on creamy lace.

Battered hats on tangled curls.

CHATTER

and soft laughter.

My granddaughter and I

are having tea.

For now,

I hold you

CLOSE

but the day must come

when I

RELEASE

you to be all

that He has planned

for you to be.

August 10

Long walks, and fr
our love alive. It
know eachothe
What promise
together mea
of our love.

August 10

Long walks, and fr
our love alive. It
know eachothe
What promise
together mea
of our love.

Even though

we are

miles apart

Our Hearts

are still

connected.

The Beauty

OF TENDERNESS

TENDERNESS
How harsh and unbearable
Our world would be without it.

She could have

brushed aside

the silent plea

for UNDERSTANDING

for SUPPORT

but she didn't.

Instead

she reached out

through her smile.

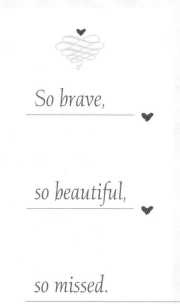

So brave,

so beautiful,

so missed.

With *Tenderness*

you cradle Kitty close

You *Coaxed* so long

And at last I heard

not just the words but

more than that your longing.

You *Needed* her.

In her own way, she's nurturing

a future *Mother.*

I must admit you're

GROWN

an adult woman

wife and mother.

Yet I keep a secret place

deep in my heart

❧ ❧ ❧

safe-tucked, eternal

and there you'll always be

my little

Girl.

She can call me
Granny, Grandmother, or Grandma

Even Nanny or Nan as she pleases

but I will always think of her
as Sunshine

because of the light that she brought
into my life.

He shows me knotted string
good for...

for fishing line
or tying up the dog
or for a kite
or maybe to lace a shoe
or...

But if I need it
he will share with me.

BAKING COOKIES

It is not merely a time

to shape and mold

dough on a metal sheet.

It is a time

to shape and mold memories

that I can carry for a lifetime

in my heart.

He LISTENS to my words and

in so doing he HEARS

a part of what is in my HEART